Emotional Healing

Sue Rose

Formerly on the staff of Trinity College, Bristol

GROVE BOOKS LIMITED
RIDLEY HALL RD CAMBRIDGE CB3 9HU

Contents

The Cover Illustration is by Peter Ashton

First Impression April 2004
ISSN 1470-8531
ISBN 1 85174 561 0

The Unity of Body, Mind, and Spirit

1

Walking recently down a street in north Oxford that was built around the time I was born, I could not help noticing how differently the properties had survived the intervening years.

Front gardens tarmacked over to make room for cars; long grass uncut and curtains only half open; a lawn littered with children's toys; crowded herbaceous border ablaze with colour; stone pots set in gravel with neatly regimented flowers and bushes. All these revealed things about their owners without a word being said.

In the same way I looked around as I walked my dog at Cortonwood, the closure of whose pit twenty years ago triggered the miners' strike. Now, superstores and hi-tech businesses lined the new through-route. The spoil heap was covered in grass, the lower slopes planted with trees and wild flowers bloomed everywhere. Ponds were created from flooded mine workings, supporting numerous varieties of plants, birds and dragonflies. New houses were springing up, and everything spoke of new hope. My eyes filled with tears at these signs of courageous 'going for life' all around, different tears from those which sprang at the sight of the dereliction and lack of any hope at nearby Grimethorpe, another one-time pit village left to its own devices when the pits also closed. Here nobody bothered to support any enterprise, and all around were signs of death and despair.

In the same way that the buildings and environment revealed the inner realities of the residents' lives, life marks us for good or ill

In the same way that the buildings and environment revealed the inner realities of the residents' lives, life marks us for good or ill—and that marking is obvious in the lines on our faces, the way we hold ourselves, even the way we dress. So much can be told from the outside about a person's attitude to himself or herself. Yet that is just the beginning of the story, because where there has been emotional damage in the past it may also have been shut away in the dark and covered by 'respectable' patterns of behaviour.

In Sickness and in Health: Is Emotional Healing Worthwhile?

All of us know from our own experience what physical illness is and have experienced the multiplicity of ways in which healing comes. Likewise many of us have direct or indirect experience of mental illness and a variety of treatments. And everyone but the newest Christian will be able to look back to times of spiritual malaise, when their experience has been anything but 'deeply rooted in the love of Christ and filled with the fullness of God' (Eph 3.17, 19).

We know that Greeks taught us to separate body, mind and spirit, but that Jewish understanding was that those areas were inextricably woven as one. The emotions—how we feel about ourselves and all that life delivers—are threaded throughout. If we are sick in any one area of our lives, the others, in a sense, come out in sympathy. Sometimes attempts are made to heal in the 'sympathy area' rather than the place where the real sickness lies, in the powerful emotional area.

Watch Anne Robinson as she deliberately plays on contestants' negative emotions about themselves to destroy their confidence and demonstrate her dominance. In contrast Johnny Wilkinson spends hours practising his place-kicking, not only to improve his technique, but so that it is automatic as he focuses so that he can cut out the number of people watching and their expectations, thus controlling his emotions so that they do not cause him to falter.

Just as cutting down on sugar, salt and fat and eating five portions of fruit and vegetables a day, plus taking regular exercise, is a general help in healthy living but cures few specific illnesses, so an overall look at one's past life and praying into what comes up is a useful general exercise towards healthy emotional living. It is also true that problems of emotional sickness may need specific attention, help from a skilled outsider and often more than a one-off visit.

So is emotional healing for a Christian simply going with the flow of the Western world, with a seasoning of prayer and Scripture?

Generations ago no-one would have thought of emotional healing outside the world of psychiatry or psychology. Similarly very few people would have looked for physical healing by spiritual means. Today's scene is very different with Christian, pagan and every sort of spiritual healing available on every street corner, advertised in every local paper and women's magazine. The same women's magazines offer articles in most issues on self-help, understanding yourself and your partner and developing your full potential.

So is emotional healing for a Christian simply going with the flow of the Western world, with a seasoning of prayer and perhaps Scripture? Or is it valid, desirable or even necessary for Christians if they are to reach maturity in their faith and its outworking?

Evidence from Scripture

The richest treasury appears within the early books of the Bible, where greed, jealousy, favouritism, fear, anger and deceit wreak havoc among the patriarchs and matriarchs of Judaism. Yet God did not spurn any of these characters. On the contrary, they were his chosen ones, carrying all their spiritual and emotional sickness, to found a nation. It is not until we come to Moses that we find someone whose emotional weakness is dealt with. Moses' big problem is his impatience and anger which culminates in murder.

Behind that lies an over-inflated sense of his own importance that thought he could single-handedly solve God's people's problems. (How many clergy and charismatically gifted lay people fall into the same trap?) These issues are dealt with in his patient learning with sheep in the desert.

ey were his chosen ones, carrying all their spiritual and emotional sickness, to found a nation

Later in the Old Testament we come across the need for a different sort of emotional healing. Isaiah despairs of his own sinfulness particularly in relation to his speaking. God provides a dramatic acting out of his cleansing so that he could be used in a prophetic ministry. Similarly Jeremiah feels utterly unable to fulfil God's call. God speaks to him directly (Jeremiah 1.5) and touches his lips thus healing him of his fears. The words God used to Jeremiah are very similar to those used in Psalm 139 which speak of God's presence and direction in the individual's life from conception to the day the words are received by the reader/listener and with it the promise to be there wherever life leads. We will come back to these verses in a later chapter.

In the New Testament, our primary source of material is in the life and teaching of Jesus himself. The encounter with Jesus is itself healing, manifesting as forgiveness for one, physical renewal for another. When a crippled man is lowered through the roof, Jesus forgives his sins first and then reveals his physical healing (Luke 5.20), but the blind man needs no explicit word of forgiveness, just healing (Mark 10.47–52). Jesus calls out the man with the withered hand where everyone can see him (Mark 3.3). His deformity made him an outcast, always feeling humiliated by the stares of others. Jesus calls

Jesus never uses God's healing to boost his own ministry

5

him into the public place to restore him, to allow him to be the centre of admiration rather than criticism.[1] Yet Jairus' daughter is healed in the privacy of her bedroom so that she is not frightened (Luke 8.54–55). Unlike some unscrupulous evangelists and healers through the years, Jesus never uses God's healing to boost his own ministry—although they retain their significance as *signs* of the inbreaking of the kingdom.

Jesus is constantly concerned with the emotional healing of others

As someone involved in emotional healing, I see that Jesus is constantly concerned with the emotional healing of others, both at the time of their physical healing and also through his everyday dealing with the disciples. As he said, 'I am come that they may have life and have it abundantly' (John 10.10). This is not the abundant life of the prosperity gospeller, full of material riches and worldly success, but the fullness that comes as it did with St Paul when he said 'I have learned to find resources within myself whatever my circumstances' (Phil 4.11, New English Bible). Just as the prophets Isaiah and Jeremiah were enabled to serve God, just as Peter, forgiven and helped through his impetuosity, was to be the leader of the new church, just as Paul, forgiven and refocused, was to be a missionary, as was John Mark, once he was over his fears, so are we met and transformed by the grace of God.

In emotional healing, one is working with paradox—an Almighty God who, despite his power, works gently in healing individuals, humans looking for healing and strength in the service of a God whose strength is made perfect in weakness. Yet a weakness that hurts other people or stultifies spiritual growth is not likely to be a source of God's strength, and needs addressing.

Anyone, or Oddballs Only?

So who could benefit from emotional healing? Anyone who is called into any sort of leadership, anyone aware of their own emotional frailty, anyone who finds their personal relationships regularly run into difficulties, or anyone who cannot break a habit or behaviour pattern. In other words, anyone who wants to grow in depth and maturity with an added understanding of others, as well as themselves. Anyone who believes that it is possible for a leopard to change its spots and is willing to humble himself enough to admit a need and to entrust himself to the hands of God, coming to him in others, will be able to grow into a new depth of maturity.

The Buildings of Our Lives

2

I have no idea where I first came across the following diagram to open up the need areas of emotional healing.

It is one I have used, adjusted and added to over the years in working with various groups.

The picture of a bungalow with loft and cellar is used to symbolize our lives and the space we live in. The comfort of our living is disturbed by pressure from all directions.

On the positive side, pressure forces us to change and to grow. So a certain amount of pressure is necessary and healthy. However, too much pressure, above our ability to handle it, is quite the opposite, causing us to function at less than optimum at one end of the scale and complete breakdown at the other.

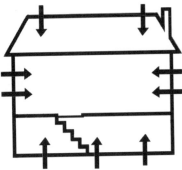

Figure 1

Where the pressure is from the society in which we live, to conform, to impress, to get on, not to appear out of date, naïve or not 'one of us,' it is comparatively easy to deal with on the level of the mind alone. It is easy, particularly with the help of an unbiased other, to look at what is being offered, to weigh its validity and then to decide whether what is offered is what is wanted from the friendship of those offering it or not.

But if the pressure is linked with that from above or below, it becomes much more complicated and needs patient healing care.

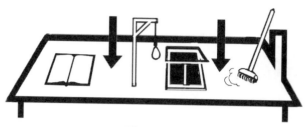

Figure 2

The pressures that come to us from *above* are all to do with law, which may be the law of God, the law of the land or the law of our family or society group. Law is usually expressed by prohibition or command, contravention of either of which brings punishment. Sticking to the law will bring safety and perhaps acceptance. It certainly leads to a controlled life, a sort of living in boxes, black or white, right or wrong decisions about life. It cuts out spontaneity and poses problems in areas that are new. Who might need healing in the meeting of legalist and sinner? Those feeling guilty, the unrepentant, those doing the judging and never looking beyond the law?[2]

Who might need healing in the meeting of legalist and sinner?

Varieties of Law

The law of God is for liberation not bondage. But religious leaders presenting their own beliefs, and the desire to control in terms that suggest that what they say is the law of God and that to disobey them is to rebel against God, will do untold harm. For example, women who are not allowed to wear make-up, dress in clothes anything like fashionable or cut their hair short, families whose members are not allowed to speak with members of their family who have 'backslidden,' people told they must speak in tongues to prove they are filled with the Spirit. An individual visiting, hearing or reading about a strongly legalistic Christian church may well feel too ashamed to darken its doors. However, those with today's highly developed *laissez-faire* attitude to most traditional church morals may miss the opportunity of seeing the chaos that comes with lack of boundaries. If we do not offer a better way than 'political correctness,' we deny the gospel and its power to heal and to change lives that are adrift or shipwrecked.

The exercise of the law of the land, as with the law of God, may be for good or ill

The law of the land gives those in authority the right to constrain the behaviour of the rest. Where the rule is benevolent the outcome is good for the majority, but where that rule is corrupt or tyrannical, the law becomes a weapon rather than a guide and so damages all who fall foul of it. The exercise of the law of the land, as with the law of God, may be for good or ill.

The law expressed by our own families, social groups, schools or churches, can be the most insidious of all in applying pressure and causing damage. Parents and teachers who instead of rejoicing at high marks only point out the one subject that has not got an A*, or the fact that no grade is higher than a C for an average child, do not encourage added effort and higher aspirations, as no doubt intended, but discouragement on the part of the child who feels that they can never satisfy.

The law expressed by our own families and social groups can be the most insidious of all in applying pressure

Jason Robinson, the Rugby international, talks in his autobiography of an incident when the club Chairman comes into the dressing room immediately after the team had lost and told them of their faults and inadequacies. The Coach rebuked him, saying that the team was well aware of their failings; right then they needed lifting up.[3] A child, who is even more sensitive, will be completely deflated by a regular diet of criticism.

Pippa Funnell, the international eventer, turned what she had learnt for herself from her psychologist to the way she trained her horses. She gave them plenty of practice at what they were good at to build their confidence to tackle their weaknesses. The law is a blunt instrument and can only go for the weaknesses. No wonder the gospel talks not only of one who sets free from sin but from guilt as well.

Sadly, many are the self-fulfilling prophesies uttered by teachers and hassled parents. 'You are stupid.' 'You're always so clumsy.' 'You are useless.' 'You will never make anything of yourself.' These words said vehemently or often enough can quickly take on the weight of law and doom people to negative beliefs that condemn them to unfulfilled lives. Similarly, declaration of stereotypical gender roles can constrain and oppress both women and men.

Continuing to Feel and to Grow

There is fascinating research into human development both in the womb and during growth into teenage years. This involves not just surges of hormones in the mother while the baby is in the womb and must pass across the placenta to the foetus, but in similar surges while the child grows up. Any extraneous happenings that occur when there is a hormone or nerve pattern surge will have a more marked effect on us than at other times. So the time in the womb, the first two or three years, the time around seven, puberty and mid to late teens will impinge on us more than any other time. For women, child bearing and menopause will have their own marked impacts, but at least in the latter case the character will be more or less fully formed so the effects will leave temporary rather than permanent markers. Not only the events themselves, but how they are interpreted decides how much damage may be done to the person. The younger the child, the more limited his or her life experience, the more likely they are to interpret in catastrophic terms. It is in these early years that opinions about the world are set and the means of coping with that world are equally set—belief systems that are extraordinarily difficult to shift later in life.[4]

The younger the child, the more likely they are to interpret in catastrophic terms

The actions and reactions of parent figures, playgroup leaders and teachers to what happens to the individual have a far greater effect for good or ill than they would imagine. The child that is given no boundaries will struggle with any form of self-discipline and find it almost impossible to cope with waiting or disappointment. The struggle may not come till school days, as the confidence of always getting what you want, at the centre of a universe which circles round you, may well fuel achievement. On the opposite end of the scale, a home that is strongly disciplinarian, or one that is shot through with fear of abuse or hedged around with the fears of an over-nervous parent will have a negative influence on the fear-restricted perceptions of the world of the growing child.

Each child grows up accepting in the first instance that what they experience in their home or school is the norm. However horrific those conditions may appear to the outsider, the child would choose to remain with the familiar rather than risk the change.[5] It is only as children grow older that they find the courage—usually to run away. If that norm is always to be hurt, then it will not be surprising if the child's behaviour is always defensive, whether that is by being aggressive and getting their hit in first, to cower and flinch thus inviting further bullying, or by shutting themselves off in a very isolated state.

Each child grows up accepting in the first instance that what the experience in their hon or school is the norm

Where wounds to the emotions, at the very beginning of the child's life, are deep and painful, they are particularly hard to deal with. Rather like having a deep-seated splinter where comfort comes by holding the site as closed as possible, so the mind closes round the emotional pain to block it off from memory altogether. The pain of opening up is greater than coping with the numbed state, so it is hardly surprising that there is reluctance to do anything. So talking to someone who has absolutely no memory of early childhood (most people have the odd memory of pre-three years and steadily larger memories after that) can indicate that something bad happened in the early days that was so traumatic that the memory has closed over the past and nothing good or ill is remembered before the event. This brings us to the last section of the house we live in.

Up from the Cellar

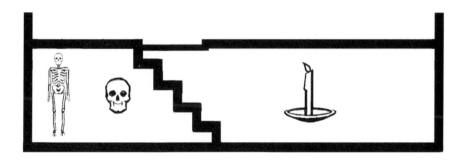

Figure 3

The cellar, the dark place where things are pushed away, is the other source of pressure on our lives. Down in the cellar are the strong emotions that are difficult to deal with. Jealousy, terror, panic and despair that all of us have the capacity to experience, are pushed there so that they do not overwhelm us. The children's book, *Where the Wild Things Are*,[6] tackles the emotions in story form in an attempt to enable children to acknowledge and handle these powerful emotions. We adults could learn much from the story. Most of us have grown up believing that such feelings are unacceptable and so they are denied and buried. They are, however, still very real as are the events that triggered them and have got buried with them.

The cellar, where things are pushed away, is the other source of pressure on our lives

The Trinity

If there is to be emotional healing for the whole person, it can be helpful to conceive of each person of the Trinity being involved:

God the Father, the creator of all, is the one most called upon in the living room of our home to create a unique living area that is safe-guarded regardless of what others say or press for. This is the safe place where what is pushed away in the loft or the cellar and causes hidden pressure can be brought out and looked at for what it is and then put into its proper place.

God the Holy Spirit is the one most called on to blow the dust off the carefully organized piles of laws—to introduce the fresh air of free-dom that the Spirit brings.

Jesus, the light of the world, needs to be allowed to take his light down into the frightening dark places of the cellar, where the darkness will no longer be able to survive and (as with the attic) enable the things that are found there be robbed of their power and put in their proper place.

All analogies have their weaknesses—this no less than any other—but as a tool it may be helpful in facilitating healing.

The Ground Around the Building

Some of the work done by Russ Parker, Directory of Acorn Christian Healing Trust,[7] on healing the land, and the Mennonites[8] in their Bridge Builders reconciliation work, would see that the area in which we live, or our church is built, may be so influenced by the bad history that has gone before that it affects all those involved there, without them having any personal responsibility. If this is the case, then it will probably need a separate act of cleansing or healing. Similarly, the surrounding culture in which a person has developed may need its own healing to enable lives lived there to thrive.

The surrounding culture in which a person has developed may need its own healing to enable lives lived there to thrive

Heavy industry, regular loss of life and life-threatening illness caused by working conditions plus unsympathetic manage-ment can blight an area with hopelessness and crush any well meaning efforts by Christians to bring the light, life and heal-ing of the gospel, even when the industry has gone. In folk memory the church is equated with the crushing cruelty of the job and the bosses. A church may be built near to an ancient battlefield and tainted in some way by the slaughter that went on. Or two parishes may be joined in a benefice unsuccessfully because no-one took notice of the fact that the two villages were on opposite sides in the Civil War or even the Wars of the Roses. The villagers can still carry inherited emotional baggage from that time.

Aidan and the Celtic missionaries claimed Northumbria for Christ and some would say the area still has awareness of the faith. Wesley brought the gospel to miners the length and breadth of the land, yet somehow there was no lasting 'God awareness.' Churches and individuals living in areas of regular oppression, or dark and sinful deeds, will find it particularly hard to flourish, as if the very ground picks up and echoes the emotions suffered. Nigel McCulloch, then Bishop of Wakefield, who spent a year taking the light of Christ into each parish and then commissioning each congregation to do the same where they were, said that there seemed to be a dead hand on some of the areas he visited. I can only speak of areas that I know, but there are certainly areas of South and West Yorkshire that would readily be called 'the land God forgot.' Some form of spiritual warfare may well be needed in the area as well as spiritual healing for the individual.[9]

3

The Stories of Our Lives

I love people's stories, whether I meet them in the flesh and hear directly or read about them second hand.

The best way to learn about emotional healing is to be part of a group with a skilled facilitator, but an appetite is whetted by reading a selection such as this. I have deliberately conflated more than one story in every case mentioned, so that although what you read is true, it cannot be ascribed to any one individual, as it is their story to tell and not mine.

Until comparatively recently, stillbirths were things to be swept away quickly, the tiny body incinerated with the placenta and parents simply told their child had not lived. No funeral service was held. No physical contact with the baby was allowed. Now, all the family are able to hold the dead baby, name it, touch and cuddle it and then have a proper funeral. It is recognized that quicker physical healing happens when the emotional needs are met. Such changes in the way the National Health Service treats patients and their families will help to limit the need for emotional healing in the future. However, that was not so for Susan and thousands like her, who had a late miscarriage and were just expected to get on as if she had experienced nothing more than a bad stomach upset.

Some twenty years later Susan was still carrying buried pain. She experienced regular bouts of depression and a general sense of unresolved failure about her life, for which she came for help. As we talked about the pattern of the depression, it became clear that she first experienced it after her miscarriage. Exploring the emptiness of that time, I asked her whether her baby had been a boy or a girl and whether she had named him. She had not consciously done so, but could immediately provide a name and therefore an identity for the lost child. We met again a week or so later, in the church, though it could have been in either of our homes—but this felt the right place to her. There we held a funeral service for the child, specially composed for the day. The work of twenty years ago was completed and she was able to move on.

The work of twenty years ago was completed and she was able to move on

Similarly, children in hospital used to be treated as solitary patients and not part of a family. Parents were seen as a nuisance and, in the worst instances, visiting was only allowed once a week or even less often if the illness was long term. It does not take much imagination to think of the fear, rejection and even desolation felt by the child. Alf's story (told with his permission) is typical.

When I was seven the panacea for sore throats and colds was a tonsillectomy. That was my fate. The location was a nearby cottage hospital, which seemed another world away. My parents abandoned me at the door, or so it seemed. The nurses and ward seemed cold and there were no other children in sight. I couldn't sleep. The night was full of moans and screams. I was scared stiff. I had no idea what was happening, even when I was wheeled into a strange smelly room and had a large rubber mask tied over my face...

It took a long time to overcome my fear of doctors and hospitals. Even now, I am apprehensive about any personal medical problems, and tend to resist ever admitting to any. But it has given me a strong desire to support those in need of medical care, and those who have to stay in hospital, even though the atmosphere and methods are very different today. They have a greater knowledge of what is happening, but need the reassurance of love and friendship—and not to feel abandoned.

If one was to look towards emotional healing in such a case, one begins with the attitudes to life, self and society that were formed and grounded by such an event. Who is carrying the blame for them—Alf, his parents, or the hospital? Does he feel it is dangerous to get close to anyone or rely on them because they will always let him down? Does he just dislike hospitals and steer clear of the medical profession as far as possible? On the surface it looks as if the latter is the case—which only becomes a problem if he refuses to go to a doctor when he is ill for fear of hospitalization. But there remains a 'niggle' about the word 'abandoned' which suggests there might be another layer to explore.

One of my parishioners was so wrapped in fear of hospitals that when she developed a back problem that quickly bent her double, she refused to go to a doctor, chiropractor or osteopath for fear of being sent to hospital. From being upright and reasonably mobile, she became doubled over with very limited mobility in a couple of days. We could never begin to talk about her condition or where the fear came from; she preferred the disability to facing her fears, so she was literally stuck.

For some children, experience of life is far more devastating. Tania was really frightened as she began to look back on her childhood, feeling that something very dark had happened. With all the publicity about the sexual abuse of children, she wondered if she was a childhood victim. That is not the sort of question you can go away and ask the family. All that could be done was to talk rationally about the worst case scenario, till the revulsion faded, then to affirm Tania's survival to date. Eventually we prayed and asked God in his good time to restore the memory to her so that it could be healed. In the event there was not sexual

We prayed and asked God in his good time to restore the memory to her so that it could be healed

abuse, just the locking away in the cupboard under the stairs with threats to chop off her fingers if she ever meddled with her father's papers again. It was still a traumatic event for a little girl in a normally peaceful family and immediate work was done to help her readjust her views of herself and her parents. The positive effect from the experience was that she was not crushed, but on the contrary, developed an iron determination not to be beaten by people or circumstances.

There are, however, numbers of people who have been abused as children, most often by members of their own family. Here is real turbulence. The people who are supposed to love you hurt you instead. You are meant to tell mummy and daddy everything, but here is a secret that must not be told. There is tremendous conflict when the abuser says that he or she loves the child, but the child hates the pain and shame of what is happening. The child tends to assume that there must be something wrong with them not to love in return. If they tell anyone then the abuse may stop, but the love will stop as well. What a terrifying dilemma for a small child, made worse if the child does risk telling the other parent and is disbelieved.

There is no quick fix to enable emotional healing in this situation, but hours of talking with a counsellor and possibly a support group will be needed before anything like healing can be found. It usually takes a long time of building trust before such a secret can be shared, so it may be done with a trusted friend or minister rather than a counsellor in the first instance. I have always found that the victim blames himself or herself for what has happened—they must be very bad, they must have done something, or they are only rubbish and deserve nothing better. The main task is to refute that lie and find a true perception. (If this is not done, the forgiveness that Christians ask from the child for the perpetrator is too readily given, after all, the child deserves no better.) Only then is it possible to admit just how bad the action, often repeated, was and that the wrong is with the perpetrator. Then the whole wrong and its ongoing effects can be explored and appropriate sorrow and anger expressed.

One boy had been abused and degraded by his father in a number of ways before being used as a rent boy by his father's friends. He had to deal with a huge amount of rage and needed the support of a group and a skilled facilitator to vent the anger safely. This was a frightening experience, but enormously cathartic for the one who had been so powerless. A long way down the line, the work is completed by forgiveness, but that does need to be right at the end of the journey. Forgiving too soon, before the depth of the injury is plumbed, means the work is not finished, merely skimmed over with poison left underneath, which will fester until it is dealt with. The importance of not offering forgiveness too soon applies to every sort of injury done to a person. On the other hand, until forgiveness is articulated the incident is not fully dealt with; the injured one remains chained to the injurer and the event.

I worked for a number of years alongside someone from the local rape crisis centre. Her experienced observation was that anyone who was raped as an adult with no previous abuse recovered comparatively easily from the experience. Those who found it hardest to recover and move on were those who had been abused in childhood. They already had a damaged view of their own identity and all the previous trauma was reawakened by the rape, even though it had previously been pushed out of their memory.

Facilitating such healing is not for the faint-hearted, nor for those who like to control others. It would be extremely irresponsible to start to unpack something that could not be completed, leaving an open wound. It would be just as irresponsible to try to control someone who has been made powerless and out of control.

Facilitating such healing is not for the faint-hearted, nor for those who like to control others

Peter, a lawyer in his thirties, had an over-protective mother, his father having died when he was ten. He was pleasant and inoffensive in his behaviour, but his body language was totally submissive. Because of that posture he had suffered some bullying, particularly in his early years at secondary school. Because he was bright and his mother wanted it, he passed his law exams with ease. Now, however, his passivity was hindering his progress in the law. He had no ability to stand up to or for his clients, but yielded to pressure. He had married someone to please his mother and was no longer sure that he loved his wife. She was getting increasingly impatient at his lack of 'get up and go.' He had met someone who thought he was wonderful. Should he leave his wife for this woman who made him feel really good about himself?

Peter felt so desperate that he was willing to undergo a long series of counselling appointments, with good gaps in between so that he could live out the truths he had discovered. He had to work on forgiving his father for dying and leaving him with no clear role model to follow into manhood. He had to work considerably longer on his relationship with his mother. In realizing that he did not have to be the substitute husband she had asked for, he was able to see what he had been robbed of in his youth. He managed to find enough indignation to fight against the smothering he had undergone under her desires and values. He had to get in touch with the rage he felt, buried deep inside. In the safety of a group for two years running he allowed himself to feel the smothering and the resulting rage. By the end, having shouted abuse at her, in her absence, at the top of his voice from a strong aggressive stance, he was able to speak as one rational adult to another and for the first time in his adult life to be a separate individual. From that position he was able to say 'no' to unrealistic demands when he got home and to tell his mother why he could not do what she wanted. Interestingly, both his marriage and his career have progressed as he has grown in confidence as the man he actually is.

His marriage and his career have progressed as he has grown in confidence as the man he actually is

Fiona worked out a freedom from a similarly dominating mother by literally picturing the limits of her life by walking them out on the carpet. She chose which side of the carpet was what person or circumstance that confined her. In turn she pushed out each boundary as far as it felt safe, deciding what she would do when she returned home to live it out. At the end of her session she moved freely in the much larger space, stretching and swinging as she went.

A group member, Jo, often closed his eyes when he talked someone—a very excluding thing to do. Eventually the group leader commented on this and out of his intervention came to light Jo's unwillingness to see or deal with anything demanding from a woman. It transpired that his mother had a difficult time at his birth. She had longed for a daughter, and when she found out that she had a son she grew hysterical. It appeared that baby Jo had decided all this was his fault and that he must never upset his mother again. (A new father said that he had always thought that a baby was born with a totally blank sheet as a brain and was amazed when he discovered by observation that this was not so. The new baby was a fully functioning being with will and desires of its own.) So it was absolutely normal behaviour for Jo to make this early decision about life. As Jo's mother taught him from a young age to be honest, he found himself in a cleft stick between being honest and not upsetting his mother. Hence his pattern of diversionary behaviour was formed. He had no idea that on the receiving end his behaviour was both rude and irritating. Within the group he had to work out whether he would climb out of the cleft by risking upsetting his mother and being honest, or whether he would remain stuck, avoiding conflict.

It is clear that a surprising number of decisions about life are made by the baby soon after birth. Yet the only really surprising thing is that one so young can form such strong opinions. The whole of life changes from the warmth and comfort of the womb, its darkness and the background of maternal body sounds. The increasing constriction of all movement stimulates the birth process. There is inevitable pain for the baby as well as the mother as the baby passes down the birth canal. Then there is the burst into the brilliant light of the delivery room, totally different noises, breathing for the first time and separating from the mother, who has always been there. Add to that the concentrated effort of birth which could last for hours and it is not surprising that the event makes a foundational impact on the child. If you also consider the extended separation that comes with the cleaning and weighing of the child and sometimes in dealing with a mother in emergency need, and the baby who has no awareness of time, other than the rhythm of the day in the womb, and the new life can start with a sense of abandonment and rejection. In Jo's case he took on board all the blame and the upset in his world.

It is clear that a surprising number of decisions about life are made by the baby soon after birth

Emotional Breakthrough

Not all occasions leading to the need for emotional healing go back this far. Jenny began to experience panic attacks to do with going outside and entering groups of people. As she was a district nurse this made life really difficult. With help she realized that the root of the trouble was her involvement in a fatal road accident when her mother was picking her up from a violin lesson. Helped with a rational starting place for an irrational fear, Jenny was able to master her fears by using controlled breathing and by having a friend who came with her and gradually encouraged her to spend increasing time on her own. She found the courage, with such support, to persevere through the panics and to lose the fear of death that had been provoked by the accident. Some eighteen months later the pattern of attacks was broken.

Fenella had been deeply in love. The family were delighted and planned the wedding with enthusiasm. A few weeks before the wedding day, she broke off the engagement and refused any contact. Fenella had a breakdown; her whole world had fallen apart and she did not know why. She was frightened to trust anyone other than her family. She resigned from her job where she had become incapable of functioning and was sure she would be given the sack. Life became a tiny box, limited to home. Her healing came through medical help, a sympathetic specialist and careful drug control. She was introduced to a community largely run by nuns. She started with a one off visit, then a weekend stay, then a fortnight, part working and partly as a guest. Finally she joined the community as a lay member. She was loved and valued, her drug dose was lowered. As she became more sure of her life, it expanded outside the community, so that when the community had to move she was able to live independently in the area. No one would begin to guess that this cheerful, outgoing person had ever been the fear-bound mouse she was years ago.

Loving prayer and care work little miracles of healing

Loving prayer and care work little miracles of healing. Skilled counselling in such a context can set people free from years of bondage. None of this does magic. God does not break us into totally new people. He crafts us as we shall see in the final chapter. The only people who may not benefit from such healing therapy are those who have mental illnesses that keep them out of touch with reality. Sadly they cannot actually hold on to the truths they have learnt, but swing back under real or perceived pressure to their old pattern of behaviour through no fault of their own. They do, however, stay healthy longer in a loving, accepting context.

Emotional Healing in the Christian Community 4

In every congregation and parish there will be a number of people who are emotionally sick and disabled.

One response is simply to expect people to pull themselves together and get on with spreading the gospel. At the opposite extreme is the response that spends all its time looking for something that needs healing and thus becoming totally self-preoccupied. Neither response is helpful.

Not every church is going to have the resources to run a full-scale healing team. We may need to share resources at a deanery, circuit or ministers fellowship level: that does demand clergy who will think bigger than their own small field, who will be willing to share their weaknesses and willing to work alongside others—in fact clergy who have risked working to get themselves more emotionally whole and unthreatened by others.

Jeremiah has a wonderful picture of God at work on his people. God called Jeremiah to go down to the potter's house, where he found the potter working on his wheel. As he was working, the vessel spoiled under his hand. Undeterred, the potter reworked it into a differently shaped vessel. Then God spoke to Jeremiah and said 'House of Israel, am I not able to do with you what I did to the pot? For you are in my hand like the clay was in the potter's' (Jer 18.1–6). That is God's normal way of working with us. He has a craftsman's hands that are sensitive to the material he is working with. He has a creator's hands that are able to make and give new life to what he makes. He has a flexible mind that is able to turn disaster into strength.

> *God has a craftsman's hands that are sensitive to the material he is working with*

Jeremiah is not alone in having beautiful pictures of God's people. Isaiah sees them as the ones in whom the Lord delights, with crowns of beauty and royal diadems (Isa 62.3–4). Or there is the other delightful picture of being hidden in the shelter of his hand and then made as the polished shaft of an arrow (Isa 49.12). If God takes such care of his children, making them into something that all may see is precious, then how careful we need to be, when people are vulnerable, to handle them with care.

The Psalmist gives us a lovely understanding of God's knowledge of and presence with the individual (Psalm 139). God was there as the cells began to divide and the body was formed in the womb—or 'intricately wrought in the depth of the earth.' Even with ultrasound imaging there is still much that is secret in all that goes on in the womb. Then as life goes on comes the awareness that there is no place in earth or heaven or hell where anyone can be away from God's spirit. In the farthest places, God's hand is there to lead and hold safe. God knows every thought, word, deed—nothing is hidden from him. Resting, working or playing, he is there—not to judge and condemn us, but to lead us in the everlasting way.

Getting Started

'Faith comes by hearing' (Rom 10.17), so a very necessary starting place is consistent preaching on the healing ministry, on dealing with the past, setting relationships right, learning to give and receive forgiveness and in growing spiritually. This will build up the congregation's expectations in the possibilities of healing and the necessity of change for all. In building a team, look for mature Christians who are trustworthy, sensitive people to whom others naturally go to share. It is a good idea to bring in a group of *Christian Listeners* to facilitate the group you have selected, ideally opening the course to other local churches.[10] Make opportunities for listeners to be available after services and at set times in the week as seems appropriate. Being listened to without being given advice, having someone give the time simply to hear what is burdening you, can be sufficiently healing in itself. Those who need more, because their needs are deeper seated, will need to go to those with counselling skills within the congregation or to any of the available healing agencies. In choosing a training organization, it is advisable to check their track record, to ensure that there is medical as well as theological representation, and check that you are happy with their theological stance.

Being listened to without being given advice can be sufficiently healing in itself

Most of the churches that have a flourishing emotional healing ministry have had regular weekends away with worship, teaching and opportunities for individual sessions, thus bringing together those who need healing and are aware of it and those who want to help the healing process. When such weekends are part of the church's annual programme, it is easier for those who recognize their need for help to ask for it.

There is no magic wand in any of this. Change takes time. If someone has carried wounds for years, one session may bring a breakthrough, but the outworking of that will take time, encouragement and patience.

Checks, Balances and Discernment

How do you learn to discern what is needed when? Read, read, read a variety of sources, all the time testing with Scripture, using your rational faculties, but at the same time keeping alert in prayer because sometimes God wants to take us beyond the experience of our reason.[11] Be aware of the dangers of pride, the allure of success, the trap of insecurity—these may be strong hidden motives for getting into a healing ministry in the church. Whereas theoretical knowledge is useful, there is no substitute for practical experience to back it up. The more practice you get, the more skilful you are likely to become. It is likely that the minister in charge of the church will not have much time for this time-consuming ministry, but experience of it on the receiving end brings with it a helpful and realistic understanding

Sources of Help

There are as many sorts of Christian healing as there are secular ones. Christian Listeners, part of Acorn Healing Trust, provide excellent courses nationwide on listening, an absolutely essential component for anyone who wants to go on to be involved in counselling.

There are many local Christian counselling centres. There are also national centres for both training and emotional healing ministry, including:

- The Crusade for World Revival, Waverley Abbey House, Waverley Lane, Farnham, Surrey, GU9 8EP. It has a strong evangelical emphasis.
- Westminster Pastoral Foundation, 25 Kensington Square, London W8 5HN. It has a mainstream liberal emphasis.
- Harnhill Centre of Christian Healing, Harnhill Manor, Cirencester, GL7 5PY.
- Acorn Christian Healing Trust, Whitehill Chase, High Street, Bordon, Hants. GU35 0AP.
- Burrswood, Groomridge, Tunbridge Wells, TN3 9PU.
- Doncaster Canaan Trust, The Manor House, Old Hexthorp, Doncaster DN4 0HY.
- Freedom in Christ Ministries—consult their web site, which can be found at www.ficm.org.uk.
- Journey into Healing, 21 Leatherhead Road, Chessington, Surrey KT19 2HN
- Wholeness through Christ, WTC Office, Wagon Road, Brightons, Falkirk, FK2 0EL

Vision, the magazine that lists retreats throughout the British Isles, provides both places and opportunities for spiritual growth to take place through spiritual direction, which may include emotional healing.

We live in a time where there are more resources than ever to enable healing and growth. That is, perhaps, because the temptations to lead a shallow selfish life have never been greater. The charge still comes to all those who are Christian to share what they have discovered and to shine as lights in a dark world.

Notes

1 Martyn Percy offers an fascinating analysis of Jesus' healing miracles entirely in terms of re-incorporation of social outcasts: see Chapter 2: 'The healing benediction: a sociological and narrative theology of miracles in the Gospels' in *Power and the Church,* (London: Cassell, 1998).

2 Those familiar with Transactional Analysis will immediately identity the contrast between Judging and Nurturing Parent, and Adapted or Free Child—see E Berne, *Games People Play* (1964).

3 *Finding My Feet* (London: Hodder & Stoughton, 2003).

4 Many theories of personal development trace the significance of these developing life stages—see, for example, D Capps, *Life Cycle Theory and Pastoral Care* (Philadelphia: Fortress Press, 1983).

5 Dave Pelzer, *A Child Called 'It'* (Orion Media, 2000). Some have questioned whether Dave Pelzer's work is truly autobiographical. The story may well be exaggerated but the clinging to home is typical of many children abused.

6 M Sendak, *Where the Wild Things Are* (London: Bodley Head, 1967).

7 Acorn Christian Foundation, Whitehill Chase, High Street, Bordon, Hants GU35 0AP.

8 London Mennonite Centre, 14 Shepherds Hill, London N6 5AQ.

9 See also, Chuck Lowe, *Territorial Spirit and World Evangelization* (OMF, 1998) for a good discussion of 'land' questions. Also the writing of Walter Wink (such as *Naming the Powers: The Language of Power in the New Testament* Philadelphia: Fortress, 1984)

10 There are several courses to train *Christian Listeners*: Acorn Christian Foundation is a good starting place.

11 Roger Hurding provides, along with much else that is enlightening, a very helpful description of each style of counselling which provides excellent background reading for anyone wanting to train or merely interested in the whole subject—see for example *Roots and Shoots,* (London: Hodder & Stoughton, 1985).